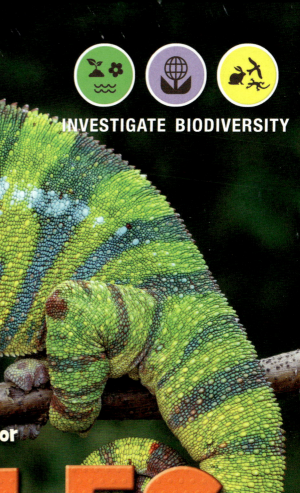

INVESTIGATE BIODIVERSITY

Rebecca Kraft Rector

REPTILES

Enslow Publishing
101 W. 23rd Street
Suite 240
New York, NY 10011
USA

enslow.com

••• Words to Know

ancestor A related human or animal that lived a long time ago.

burrow A hole in the ground where animals live.

extinct No longer living.

habitat A kind of place where plants or animals live normally.

hibernate To sleep during a period of cold.

scales Small, hard plates that cover a reptile's body.

shed To fall off naturally.

species A group of plants or animals that are like each other.

webbed Having skin between the toes.

••• Contents

Meet the Reptiles

What is a reptile? Reptiles are animals with **scales**. Reptiles breathe air. They have backbones.

Dinosaurs were reptiles. Dinosaurs lived millions of years ago. They are now **extinct**.

Kinds of Reptiles

There are five kinds of reptiles. Snakes and lizards are one group. Turtles are another. Alligators and crocodiles are one more group. Tuataras are the fourth group. They look like lizards. Tuataras can only be found in New Zealand.

The Fifth Group

Scientists say birds are reptiles. It is because they have dinosaur **ancestors**. But birds do not share many reptile features. So they are not discussed in this book.

Reptiles come in all shapes and sizes! But all of them are covered with scales.

The Komodo dragon is the largest and heaviest lizard in the world.

There are about 6,000 **species** of reptiles. This does not include birds. Most reptiles are snakes or lizards. There are more than 2,500 species of snakes. About 3,000 species of lizards exist. There are about 250 species of turtles. There are about 20 species of alligators and crocodiles. There are only two species of tuataras.

Reptile Bodies

Reptiles are not all the same size. The smallest reptile is the dwarf gecko. It is less than one inch (25.4 millimeters) long. Some large snakes and crocodiles grow to 30 feet (9 meters).

Most reptiles have four legs. Snakes have no legs. They move by pushing and pulling against the ground.

All reptiles have scales. Reptile scales are a hard layer of skin. Scales protect the body. They help keep in moisture.

A snake sheds its outer skin all at once. This skin left on a branch is still in the shape of the snake.

Fast Fact

Snake scales lie flat. Snakes feel smooth. Lizards usually have scales that overlap. Most lizards feel rough.

Turtle shells are made of bony scales. Alligators and crocodiles are covered in large scales.

Reptiles **shed** their scales as they grow. Some shed a few scales at a time. Snakes shed all their scales at once.

Life Cycles

Most reptiles lay eggs. Some snakes and lizards have live babies. Sea turtles can lay more than one hundred eggs. Crocodiles have about fifty eggs. Smaller reptiles may lay only one egg.

First Comes the Egg

Reptiles lay their eggs on dry land. Even water turtles come to shore to lay eggs. The eggs have hard shells. They are tough and leathery. Many reptiles make a nest or hole for their eggs. They lay the eggs. Then they cover them up. They leave the eggs behind. Some reptiles stay with their eggs.

This female python is protecting her eggs by curling up on them.

Cobras and pythons curl around their eggs. Female crocodiles guard their eggs. Some lizards called skinks also take care of their eggs.

Most reptile babies are born in eight to twelve weeks. This is true for both those born from eggs and from live births. If the nest was buried, the babies must dig their way out.

Growing Up

Reptile parents do not usually stay with their babies. However, female crocodiles and alligators protect and care for their young. They may carry babies on their backs. Sometimes they carry babies in their mouths.

Most reptiles grow quickly. Some reptiles are adults after four months. Some reptiles take nine years to become adults. Most stop growing

A boy inspects a giant Galapagos tortoise. These tortoises can live for 100 to 150 years.

A baby crocodile takes a ride in its parent's mouth.

when they are adults. Crocodiles and alligators continue growing until they die.

Most reptiles have long lives. Turtles often live more than 30 years. Some turtles have lived for 150 years. Crocodiles can live for 20 years. Large snakes also live a long time.

Home Sweet Home

●●● Reptiles live in almost every **habitat** on Earth. Some live in hot deserts. Some live near the cold Arctic Circle. No reptiles live in Antarctica.

Need for Heat

Most reptiles live where it is warm. Humans make their own body heat. Reptiles must take in heat from the world around them. Often reptiles lie in the sun to get warm. They go underground to cool off. If the weather is cold, reptiles will **hibernate**. Many reptiles hibernate in **burrows**. Turtles may dig into the mud under the water.

The tuatara can live with cold temperatures. A few snakes and lizards can live in the Arctic region.

A rare tuatara comes out
of its burrow.

Land and Sea

Most snakes and lizards live on land. They may live in mountains, forests, or deserts. Many live underground. Some live in trees. Sea snakes live in the water. Anacondas are water snakes.

Most turtles live in the water. Most do not like salty water. They live in ponds or lakes. Sea turtles live in the oceans. The leatherback turtle is a huge sea turtle. It can grow longer than 6.5 feet (2 meters). Some turtles live on land. Land turtles are often called tortoises.

A lizard called a lace monitor suns itself on a tree branch to get warm.

A banded sea snake glides through the water.

Fast Fact

All reptiles have lungs. This means they breathe air. Reptiles that live in the water must come up for air.

Alligators and crocodiles live in the water. Alligators live in fresh water. Crocodiles like salty water. Both reptiles can run on land for short distances.

What Do Reptiles Do?

● ● ● Reptiles work hard to stay alive. They look for food. They protect themselves. Many animals want to eat them.

Finding Food

Most reptiles eat meat. A few eat plants. Iguanas and land tortoises eat plants. Sea turtles eat water plants. Kelp and algae are examples of water plants.

Fast Fact

Alligators have eyes on top of their heads. Their bodies hide underwater. But they can still watch for danger and for food.

A sidewinder rattlesnake makes its way across the desert.

Reptiles search for their food. Most move on four legs. Snakes push and pull against the ground. Sea turtles have **webbed** feet. The webs help them swim. Sea snakes, crocodiles, and alligators use their tails to push through the water.

Reptiles use their senses to find food. Reptiles have a special structure in their mouth or nose. It helps them taste and smell. Lizards, alligators, and crocodiles can hear sounds. Snakes and turtles cannot. But they can feel vibrations. Snakes cannot see well. But they can sense the body heat of other animals.

A basilisk lizard can run across the water to get away from a predator.